PARENT'S GUIDE TO THE NEW YORK STATE 4TH GRADE TESTS

Cynthia and Drew Johnson

Simon & Schuster

Kaplan Publishing
Published by Simon & Schuster
1230 Avenue of the Americas
New York, NY 10020

For bulk sales to schools, colleges, and universities, please contact Vice President of Special Sales, Simon & Schuster Special Markets, 1230 Avenue of the Americas, New York, NY 10020

Editor: Maureen McMahon
Page Designer: Gumption Designs
Cover Design: Cheung Tai

Manufactured in the United States of America

November 1999

10 9 8 7 6 5 4 3 2

Library of Congress Cataloging-in-Publication Data is available.

ISBN 0-684-86961-6

All of the practice questions in this book were created by the authors to illustrate question types. They are not actual test questions. For more useful information on the New York State Testing Program, including sample questions and answers, visit the New York State Education Department's Student Tests and Assessments Web site at **www.nysed.gov/ciai/assess.html**.

CONTENTS

Acknowledgments

The authors would like to thank Lenor Medina and Karen Daley for their help in reviewing this book and making suggestions. The authors would also like to thank Maureen McMahon and Lori DeGeorge for their enormous contributions toward making this book a reality.

The publisher would like to thank Michael Carter, Mildred Ramos, Deborah Walker-Dudley, Carole Lippold, Cynthia Lapsley, Lillian Hernandez, and Frank White for their guidance and advice.

INTRODUCTION

Although several years have passed since you were nine years old, your fourth-grade experience and your child's are probably not very different. There are still spelling bees at school, dodgeball games at recess, and giggling fits during class in which students try to stop laughing, but just can't. These are all memories you can share with your child. However, the memory of spending weeks in intensive preparation for two three-day-long standardized tests is one your child will have all on his or her own.

The tests in question are the New York English Language Arts and Mathematics tests for grade four. Described as the Elementary Level Tests, the fourth-grade exams, which roughly two hundred thousand children take annually, go hand in hand with the Eighth Grade Intermediate Level Tests. The fourth-grade Math and English exams are each a mixture of multiple-choice questions, short open-ended questions, and extended open-ended questions. The English exam also contains a passage the teacher reads out loud on which the children take notes and then write two short responses and one extended response. Critics of the test could state that some IRS forms are easier to understand than this test format. While this may be true, if you and your child familiarize yourselves with the test structure, your child will not be confused or frustrated by the test format and will instead approach the three-day exams with the confidence of a veteran accountant handling a 1040EZ form.

How the Elementary Level Tests Were Born

Although these fourth-grade tests cover only math and reading, a little history will help put the test in perspective. In 1995 the New York State Education Department created a detailed outline of the curriculum requirements for all subjects from prekindergarten to high school. These massive volumes languished in obscurity, however, since they did not correspond to the types of questions being asked on the statewide tests. A year earlier the Educational Board of Regents had approved a plan to revise the tests, and so the task of combining the detailed curriculum with the new test format fell to Education Commissioner Richard P. Mills. Mr. Mills made testing at all grade levels the focal point of his agenda, toughening the academic standards and changing the format of the tests from a purely multiple-

> "It's not fair to graduate children without the knowledge or skills to make it in the world. We are setting them up for failure."
>
> —Richard Mills

choice affair to a three-day, diverse-question setup. The first wave of students who took these new tests showed the effects of the higher standards: 52 percent of all New York fourth-graders failed the English exam in 1999 (results for the three-day math test, given later in the year, were not yet available at the time of this printing). In New York City the new test took an ever greater toll, as only 33 percent of all Big Apple students received a passing grade. These massive failure rates made headlines statewide and, understandably, caused widespread concern (and finger-pointing) among parents and educators. Some critics claim the tests were too hard, others that the students were poorly prepared. The debate continues.

One thing seems clear: low scores do not mean these tests will be made easier or eliminated. The emphasis on standardized testing at all levels is growing stronger, not weaker. In fact, there were even plans to start testing all New York second-graders, although these were eventually scrapped. With "accountability" the pervasive theme in national education, more and more states are setting academic standards and then rewarding or punishing schools depending on whether they achieve these standards.

What's at Stake?

With so much emphasis being placed on these two tests, you'd think the fourth-graders who take them should be given the right to vote as a reward (at least in state elections). Quite a bit is at stake, for both the child and the school district. The state ranks all schools based on how well their students fared on the exam. Schools that do badly may have superintendents, principals, or teachers fired. Underperforming schools land on the state list called Schools Under Registration Review and may be closed if improvement is not seen on the tests and in other academic areas.

As for the individual fourth-grader, a plan is in place to require all students who fail the English portion of the test to take remedial instruction. For instance, the New York City school board strongly urged sixteen thousand fourth-graders who failed the English test in 1999 to take summer school classes to improve their skills. Mills has proposed that all students who fail be required to retake the test, but this plan has not yet been enacted. Currently, each school district must decide whether students who fail the fourth-grade tests can be promoted to the fifth grade, so the fate of the thousands of students who failed in 1999 will be determined by geography.

How You Can Help

Many of you are already aware of how important the fourth-grade tests are to your son or daughter, which is why you picked up this book in the first place. While your child's teacher is probably already doing some exam-related work in the classroom, nothing is better for your child than tutoring from someone she trusts. Since Mr. Rogers is busy this time of year, that person will have to be you. In this book are all the facts, tips, questions, activities, and advice you will need to help your child succeed on the fourth-grade tests. The *Parent's Guide to the New York State 4th Grade Tests* lets you know exactly what skills are being tested on the Math and Reading tests, gives you test-taking strategies to make taking these tests easier, and tells you exactly how to teach your child these skills and strategies. By analyzing and discussing the test in detail, our goal is not only to provide you and your child with the basic knowledge she needs to excel on the test, but to instill a sense of confidence through familiarity, since feeling confident and prepared for these three-day affairs is a key factor in how a student fares on the tests.

After reading this book, both you and your child should feel ready to take on the tests first, and then the fifth grade. Though that feeling might not do you any good while you are at work, it will do wonders for your kid.

Testing en Español—and Other Special Cases

The current criteria for whether your child can take these tests in another language are somewhat tricky. It all depends on how your child does on another exam: the English Reading test. If your child scores above the thirtieth percentile on this test, he has the option of taking the Math test in Spanish, Chinese, Haitian Creole, or Russian, if his language teacher approves. If your child scores at or below the twenty-ninth percentile on an English Reading test and has been enrolled in the United States for five years or less, then he may be exempted from taking the English test. However, this exemption request must be reported through the Local Education Accountability Program.

All parents of Special Education students should clarify their child's test-taking rights with their local school districts.

Chapter One THE As, Bs, Cs, AND Ds OF GOOD TEST-TAKING

Understanding the Elementary Level Tests Is Half the Battle

Does the mere sight of a No. 2 pencil cause your child to break into a cold, trembling sweat? Are the words *multiple choice* or *short essay* invariably followed by a thin, keening shriek or forlorn wail? If the answer to either of these questions is *yes*, then it's time you faced the facts: when it comes to taking standardized tests, your child is just like everyone else.

The vast majority of Americans experience some fear and nervousness before taking a big test. It is only natural that a nine- or ten-year-old would feel anxious when faced with a test that might cause her to have to take summer school or maybe even be held back a grade. Sure, a few folks out there are perfectly calm when faced with exams, but they are all either hopelessly insane or currently making a livelihood writing test-preparation materials.

Let your kid know that it is normal to be nervous about the unknown, but that the more he knows about the New York Math and English tests, the less nervous he will feel. All the information and all the techniques we will cover in this book will ease your child's nervousness and replace it with confidence by making that "unknown"—in this case, the exams—familiar and manageable. Test anxiety almost invariably leads to a lower test score, so it is important that you boost

The Breakdown

English Language Arts
(three days of testing)

Session 1: 5 reading passages, 28 multiple-choice questions. 45 minutes.

Session 2: Part 1: Listen to a passage—2 short responses, 1 long response (basic essay format). 30 minutes.

Part 2: Write a composition (definitely essay time!). 30 minutes.

Session 3: Read 2 related passages—3 short responses, 1 long response. 60 minutes.

Mathematics
(also three days of testing)

Session 1: 30 multiple-choice questions. 40 minutes.

Session 2: 7 short open-ended questions, 2 extended open-ended questions. 50 minutes.

Session 3: 7 short open-ended questions, 2 extended open-ended questions. 50 minutes.

your child's confidence level about the exam. Just understanding the basic format of both these exams can be empowering, as the Math test changes from a scary hurdle that must be jumped and becomes simply "a test taken in three sessions, with the first session filled with multiple-choice questions while the last two sessions have short and long extended-response questions."

The importance of knowing what to expect was clearly illustrated in 1999, when so many fourth-graders faced—and failed—the Grade 4 English test. Most likely, the new, unexpected format unnerved them. It was not that New York fourth-graders do not know how to write a short essay; rather, the test format was so unfamiliar to them that they had no idea what they were supposed to write, or when they were supposed to write it. When faced with an unexpected, open-ended question, even most adults can become unsure of themselves.

Learning about question types and little details, such as which math questions are worth two points and which are worth three points, serves a dual purpose for the tests: it provides your child with useful information, and it takes away the fear-of-the-unknown aspect of the test. This principle is the foundation of successful test preparation:

THE END-OF-SENTENCE GAME

For a fun way to quiz your child about basic Elementary Level Test facts, try playing this game. For one evening (or longer), try to sneak in simple questions at the end of ordinary sentences, so that "Please pass the potatoes" becomes "Please pass the potatoes if you know how many multiple-choice questions there are in the first Math session." Your child has to answer as quickly as possible, and correctly as well. The game can be one-player, with your child working to get as many right in a row as possible, or it can be two-player, so that your child can say, "Dear parental unit, would you please read me a bedtime story and describe the format for questions on the second day of the English exam?"

Familiarity leads to confidence.

Think of the fourth-grade tests as that haunted house on the end of your street. By knowing nothing about it, your child has only the horror stories about the children who went inside never to be seen again. Your job as a parent is to guide your child through the exams during the day, showing how the scary noise coming from upstairs is caused by a rusty blind, and that beyond the usual dangers associated with an old house (loose floorboards, a rickety staircase), there is nothing about the place to worry about. If you can replace the anxiety and stress your child feels about the fourth-grade tests with a feeling of confidence, you will have done your child a great service.

Why Cosmos N'Deti, Former Boston Marathon Winner, Would Probably Do Well on the Elementary Level Tests

Although Mr. N'Deti, a world-class marathon runner, has probably not had as much work with fractions as your child has recently, he is skilled in one crucial test-taking area: *pacing*. Knowing that he's going to run twenty-six miles, N'Deti picks a nice, consistent speed at which to run and keeps at that pace throughout the entire race. What he *doesn't* do, and what you should not allow your child to do, is spend too much time in any one area or run out of gas before the race is over.

Since a variety of question types are on these exams, how much time your child should spend per question will be covered in greater detail in the Math and Reading chapters. However, the main idea you must pass on to your child now is not to spend too much time ever on any one question. Perseverance is a noble trait, but on a standardized test, spending half your time answering one multiple-choice question is tantamount to standardized-test suicide. Your child should stay focused on the task at hand and never get too flustered by any one question. One or two small breaks during each section is fine if your child feels her brain is getting strained. Tell her to put the pencil down, stretch out her hands and arms, take some deep breaths, and then pick up the pencil and finish the test. If your child comes to a question she does not understand, tell her to think of this guideline:

> ***Spend about one minute trying to figure out the question;
> then, using the techniques taught in this book, take an
> educated guess and move on.***

The fourth-grade tests do not require perfection. There are only two real scores: pass or fail. To pass, students need to get about two-thirds of the questions right, so it is never worth their while to spend fifty minutes on one question that's stumping them, only to be so mentally fatigued that they do poorly on the rest of the exam. Certainly, you don't want to encourage your child to do less than her best, but she must realize that no one question is so important that it is worth getting bogged down on and upset over. Some questions always seem baffling. Throughout the rest of this book, we'll show you how to show your kid how to make good guesses, keep her cool, and stay on pace when faced with a stumper.

In addition to telling your child not to get stuck on one question, you can also encourage the "two-pass" approach to test-taking. On the first pass through a section, your child should answer only those questions she can handle quickly and easily, skipping over any questions that leave her confused or require a lot of thought. Seeing a bunch of ovals filled in right away often gives students a quick boost of confidence. On the second pass, tell your child to go a little slower, use the process of elimination (a technique we'll discuss in a moment) to cross out any incorrect choices, and then take a guess and move on.

To help illustrate the importance of pacing, here's a little "test-prep fable" you might share with your child:

KAPLAN'S TEST-PREP FABLES: THE TALE OF ISHMAEL THE SNAIL

Call him Ishmael the Snail. When all the fish signed up for the annual aquarium obstacle-course race, no one gave him much of a chance, but Ishmael was confident of his abilities. The starting gun sounded, and all the contestants took off. The goldfish Ahab took the lead, but she got caught up on a whale of an obstacle early on. She couldn't figure out how to get around it, and she never finished the race. The two Ya-Ya loaches were also fast, but they made too many mistakes. They kept swimming under the hurdles instead of over them, and they skipped some obstacles completely, so they wound up being disqualified. The gourami started out at a good clip, but he fell fast asleep around the plastic plant and Ishmael passed him up. Ishmael ran the entire course at a steady, constant pace, rarely making mistakes, and when the final results were tallied, Ishmael was the winner. As his reward, Ishmael was named king of the aquarium. He now lives in a plastic castle and rules the fish wisely and fairly.

Moral: A steady pace wins the race.

Edgar Allan P.O.E. for English and Math Session 1

One of the biggest advantages in taking a multiple-choice test is that you don't always have to know the correct answer. Think about it: the answer is already there, staring you in the face. If you find all the incorrect answers and eliminate them, you will get the question right. The *process of elimination* technique, known as P.O.E. in test-taker's lingo, is one that good test-takers use instinctively, but which anyone can learn to do with practice. It is especially helpful on the New York tests because there is no guessing penalty. You see, on some standardized tests, a fraction of a point is deducted from a student's final score for every question answered incorrectly. This is known as a *guessing penalty,* and it is meant to discourage random guessing. On the New York tests, no points are deducted. A wrong answer simply results in zero credit, not negative credit, so your child has nothing to lose and everything to gain by making good guesses on questions he is having trouble answering. And P.O.E. is the key to good guessing.

To demonstrate the effectiveness of this technique, see if your child can answer the following question.

1. How old are the authors of this book?
    A.   4 years old
    B.   29 years old
    C.   35 years old
    D.   126 years old

If this weren't a multiple-choice question, your child would have little to no chance of getting the right answer. However, as it stands, she should have narrowed the choices to either B or C, giving her a fifty-fifty shot of guessing correctly. Since, as we mentioned, there is no penalty for guessing, she should then pick either B or C and move on to the next question.

Use process of elimination to cross out incorrect answer choices.

Perhaps the hardest part about using P.O.E. is knowing when to use it. In the above question, for example, how would you know that A and D were incorrect? You could say you used common sense, and that would be a valid answer. In many ways common sense translates to a basic understanding of what the question is asking, and therefore what the possible answers could be. Ask your child the question below, and help her use common sense to get a general idea of what the answer will be.

> Thomas had $4.00, but he gave half of his money away
> to his friend Jeremy for a plastic bucket. Then Thomas
> gave away half of his remaining money to buy some
> gum. How much money does Thomas now have?

Before looking at the answer choices, ask your child the following questions:

Could Thomas now have more than $4.00?

Could Thomas have no money at all?

Could Thomas have $2.00?

The answer to all these questions is no. The last question is probably the toughest. But even if that question is confusing to your child, she could still look at the answer choices and eliminate some incorrect responses.

> A. $4.00
> B. $2.00
> C. $1.00
> D. $0.00

Why would answer choice A even be there? The test designers put it there to catch the careless student. They know many students often glance at a question, feel unsure of how to work the problem, then just pick a number from the question that appears in the answer choices. Using the process of elimination—and thinking about what the question is really asking—can help your child avoid these mistakes.

P.O.E. can also be used on the fourth-grade Reading exam. The incorrect choices are generated the same way they are in the above question: words are taken from the reading passage and placed out of context as an answer choice. Students who remember seeing the words in the passage mistakenly pick them as an answer choice, never questioning whether the answer makes sense. Here's an adaptation of a recent fourth-grade reading question:

1. Where did Farmer Ike keep his cows?
   A. in the barn
   B. in a fenced-in pasture
   C. at a fruit stand
   D. in his house

Which of these choices can be eliminated? Hopefully, your child will recognize C and D as unlikely correct answers. C is wrong because stacking cows into pyramids is much harder than stacking apples and oranges, and D is unlikely because no farmer likes to have dinner interrupted by a stampede crashing through the kitchen. Still, these were actual answer choices, because the words *fruit stand* and *house* appeared in the reading passage.

So far, all of the examples of P.O.E. have dealt with multiple-choice questions, which comprise only the first third of each test. While P.O.E. is not the best tool to use when writing an essay, the technique can be used for some open-ended math questions. Although these open-ended questions are not as amenable to P.O.E. as a multiple-choice question, many problems in Math Sessions 2 and 3 are multistep questions requiring the student to do more than one computation. On questions such as these, P.O.E. is an excellent tool to either find the correct answer or at least do work that deserves partial credit. For example:

Michael reached into his desk and brought out these 7 pens.

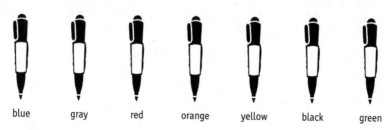

| blue | gray | red | orange | yellow | black | green |

Michael used one of the pens to color on a map. Use the clues on the next page to find out which color Michael used.

Clues

It has less than 6 letters, but more than 3 letters in its name.

It is *not* the first or the last pen.

It is not next to the red pen.

What color pen did Michael use?

Explain the steps you used to find your answer.

In essence, this question is nothing but a three-step P.O.E. question, although instead of using common sense to eliminate answer choices, you use the clues given to you. With the first clue, you can eliminate red, orange, and yellow. The second clue knocks out blue and green, and the third clue eliminates gray, leaving only black. Even if your child messes up one of the clues and ends up with the wrong final answer, by describing which colors he eliminated and why, he could earn half credit on the question.

Have an Answer for Everything

Suppose your child comes to a multiple-choice math question that she can't figure out at all. She spends some time looking over the answer choices to see if there are any she feels she can cross out, but nothing comes to mind. Process of elimination fails her. Should she leave this question blank and move on to the next question? The answer is "No, no, no, no, no, a thousand times no!" Again, there is no guessing penalty on the fourth-grade exams, so every question must be filled in, even if it means random guessing instead of educated guessing (although educated guessing using P.O.E. is always better, of course). Advise your child to:

1. Look for ways to work the problem using the correct math or reading skill. (On the open-ended questions, be sure to write down what skill you are applying, as discussion of the right technique could earn partial credit.)

2. Use P.O.E. to cross out incorrect answer choices.

3. Guess and move on, knowing that your test grade does not depend on every little question.

If your child needs further convincing about the benefits of guessing, you might try telling the following story:

KAPLAN'S TEST-PREP FABLES: THE STORY OF KRONHORST THE FUZZY CHIHUAHUA BUNNY

Early in his life Kronhorst was just like all the other bunnies. He enjoyed carrots, frolicking in a pasture, and hopping up and down to his heart's content. One day, though, the Bunny Master came to all the bunnies in the world and said, "Okay, it's time you all got ears." (This happened a long time ago, when all bunnies were earless.) The bunnies had several choices to pick from: "long and floppy," "really long and floppy," "and "tastefully long and floppy," just to name a few. Every bunny made a choice except Kronhorst, who couldn't pick between "cute and floppy" or "trippily floppy."

Not making a choice was the worst thing that ever happened to Kronhorst, because from that point on everyone he met always mistook him for a fuzzy Chihuahua. "Look at that way too hairy Chihuahua!" people would cry, at which point Kronhorst would have to explain that he was a bunny. People would then ask, "But where are your ears?" Needless to say, Kronhorst got pretty tired of these conversations, as well as the endless invitations to the Hair Club's Annual Dog Show.

Moral: Answer every question on the exam or people will confuse you with a fuzzy Chihuahua.

While this advice is crucial for both multiple-choice Math and English sections, it is no less important on the essays and open-ended math questions. There might be one open-ended math question that will look to your child as if it came directly from the Math Institute of Neptune. If so, tell your child to write *Neptune* next to it and come back later if there's time. However, he must not write *Neptune* more than once. On all other math questions, your child should give it his best attempt and make sure to document his attempt well. Who knows? Your child's guess might be the correct solution, or it might display enough sound math principles to garner partial credit.

The Number One and Only Child in the Class

Students are naturally leery of answering a question they do not feel they know the answer to, and they prefer not to say anything unless they are absolutely sure they are right. Teachers see this all the time in classrooms: children refuse to raise their hands and offer answers to questions because they are afraid of being embarrassed by a wrong answer. Unfortunately, this habit will hurt your child's test score. So explain to her that on these exams, she should act as if she is the only student in her favorite teacher's class, and if she does not answer, the teacher has to just stand there until she does.

The Only Way to Avoid Mental Mistakes

Nothing is gained by trying to solve any of these problems in your head. While it is impressive if your child can multiply big numbers without using pen and paper, it's not required for the Math exam. In fact, it even works against his score. Get your child into the habit of writing down all his work on math problems and jotting down the main idea of a reading passage as he goes through it. Kids can eliminate a slew of careless errors simply by writing down their work. For many children, writing things down helps them clarify the material. Writing down work during practice sessions also makes for a better learning experience: if your child misses a question, at least you can go back together and see what the problem was.

Write down your work whenever possible.

As stated throughout this chapter, writing down your work is crucial on the open-ended math questions. To illustrate this, read the following example and then see how Imperious Student A and Well-Behaved Student B responded.

> Jonathan had $5.00 at the start of the day. At noon, he gave half of his money to Gwendolyn, and at 3:00 he lost $0.50 in a vending machine.
>
> How much money did Jonathan have at the end of the day? Explain your answer.

Imperious Student A:
Jonathan had two bucks *because I say he did. Now all must bow to the brilliance of Student A!!*

Well-Behaved Student B:
Starting out with five dollars, Jonathan gave half, or $2.50, away, meaning he only had three dollars left. Then he lost 50 cents, so $3.00 - $0.50 = $2.50.

Not only is Student A a megalomaniac, he is also no better than Student B on this question. Student A provided the right answer with an inadequate solution, earning A only 1 point out of 2. Student B has the wrong answer but the right explanation, so B gets 1 point as well. Since there are 18 open-ended questions on the entire Math portion of the exam, garnering a few points via properly showing his work could significantly boost your child's final score.

This technique of writing down your work is just as helpful throughout the Reading section as it is on the Math section. On the multiple-choice reading passages, have your child take whatever notes about the passage she is comfortable with, ranging from writing down the main idea to summarizing each paragraph. You don't want your child to spend a lot of time looking for the perfect phrase to describe the Reading section, but writing down any thoughts she has about the passage will help your child understand the passage better. Since many reading questions are testing just how well your child understands the action in the reading paragraph, any notes your child writes to aid her reading comprehension should lead to an improved score. Writing down notes becomes absolutely critical for Sessions 2 and 3 of the Reading section, so any practice your child gets in this area can only help improve her score.

"'Twas the Night before the Tests . . ."

Make sure your child feels confident and well rested on the days of the test. Hopefully, this means keeping the nightly routine as regular as possible. You might want to schedule some sort of activity for the nights before and during the test, but it should *not* be cramming. Trying to jam in tons of information on the night before a test session is not conducive to a child's test-taking confidence, and it should be avoided.

A positive attitude is more important than any one fact.

This is especially important for the interim nights after Sessions 1 and 2. If your child feels she did badly on the test that day, do everything you can to change her attitude before the next morning. Tell your child that if she followed the techniques in this book and the ones that she learned in her classroom, then her score will not be as bad as she might think it is.

If your child does want to review for a while, stick to the basics, asking questions about the test format and general test-taking strategies. These will come in handier than reviewing any particular part of the Math or Reading section. Also, your child will probably answer most of the general test-format questions correctly, which will boost her confidence. What you do not want is to have your child stumped by a series of questions, because then she will go into the exam the next day thinking she is going to do badly.

Here's a handy list of pointers for the time before an exam:

THINGS TO DO BEFORE THE EXAM

1. Make sure your child gets adequate rest.

2. Give your child a healthy, adequate breakfast.

3. Let your child have any medication only if he takes that medication regularly.

4. Participate in some activity at night that is fun for your child but not too taxing. (Watching a movie on the VCR or playing board games are two ideas.)

5. Give your child words of encouragement right before she goes to take the test.

You get the main idea. Send your kid to school relaxed and positive, and don't do anything to upset her normal rhythm. Some things that would *definitely* upset her normal rhythm and should be avoided are:

THINGS NOT TO DO BEFORE THE EXAM

1. Send her to bed earlier than usual, because she will just lie in bed thinking about the test.

2. Let your child have any noncritical medication (such as over-the-counter cold or allergy medicine) that will cause drowsiness or muddled thinking.

3. Decide to unwind by watching the midnight triple-header of Nightmare on Elm Street I, II, *and* III.

4. Decide that the morning of the test is the perfect time to explain to your child how big the national debt really is, and what that will mean to her.

Review

The Main Points

1. Understand the format of both the Math and English exams and be comfortable with it.

2. Maintain a consistent pace throughout the test, and don't let any single question get you flustered.

3. Use the process of elimination whenever possible.

4. Answer every question.

5. Write down all work to avoid foolish mental mistakes and to earn possible partial credit.

6. Make sure you are relaxed and positive on test day.

Questions to Ask Your Child

1. What's the moral of "Ishmael the Snail"? *A steady pace wins the race.*

2. Ask general questions about the test format until your child answers the queries easily. *How many questions on the multiple-choice Reading section? How many answer choices for every question?*

3. What does P.O.E. stand for? *Process of elimination.* Why would you want to use P.O.E.? *Because finding incorrect answers and crossing them out gives you a better chance of answering a question correctly.*

4. What's the moral of "Kronhorst the Fuzzy Chihuahua"? *Answer every question on the test or be mistaken for a Chihuahua with a hair problem.*

5. When should you solve questions in your head? *Never!*

6. Who will love you no matter how you do on these exams? *Your parents, of course!*

Chapter Two ENGLISH LANGUAGE ARTS

Getting a Read on the Reading Section

As you will learn later in this chapter, "finding the main idea" is an important technique to help students solve questions correctly. But before this technique is applied to specific test questions, it should be applied to the fourth-grade English Language Arts test first. This exam lasts three days, with a variety of formats: What's the main idea of this test?

In the view of the New York State Education Department, students are being tested on three main ideas, or Learning Standards. They are:

1. **Information and Understanding.** *Students collect data, facts, and ideas; discover relationships, concepts, and generalizations; acquire and interpret information.* In other words, your child is able to read a sentence like "The quick brown fox jumped over the lazy dog" and understand what it means well enough to answer questions like "What color is the fox?" or "Does the dog appear to have a job?"

2. **Literary Response and Expression.** *Students will read and listen to texts and relate these texts to their own lives; they will develop an understanding of the diverse social, historical, and cultural dimensions of the work; and they will be able to write down their own thoughts and ideas in proper English.* To paraphrase, students will read the sentence like "The quick brown fox jumped over the lazy dog" and be able to write an essay "describing any experiences you might have had with a quick brown fox and what you learned from it" or write several paragraphs wherein your child describes "some possible reasons why the dog is so lazy, and what could be done about it."

3. **Critical Analysis and Evaluation.** *As listeners and readers, students will analyze experiences, ideas, information, and issues presented by others; they will use proper English and be able to convey their own opinions and judgments on experiences, ideas, information, and issues.* Translation: your child is able to write essays on topics like "why a certain brown fox needs to slow down before someone gets hurt."

Not every test session covers all three Learning Standards. Session 1, consisting of reading passages followed by multiple-choice questions, deals only with Learning Standards 1 and 2. For the most part, Standard 1 is stressed more than 2 in this session, so you can tell your child that on the first day of testing, the emphasis is on whether students can understand and answer questions about what they read. A little bit of independent thought is required to do this, but not as much as for the next two sessions.

The second day of testing, Session 2, focuses only on Literary Response and Expression. So your child has to be in the mood to say what is on her mind, or else that day is going to be a *long* day. This is not an easy thing to do. Fourth graders have little experience with literary interpretation, and many children, understandably, are reluctant to come up with their own ideas about a story and then express them eloquently in a time-constrained, high-pressure moment. Nevertheless, that is the key to a good score on Sessions 2 and 3. Explain to your child that if she hears a fable during the listening section, it is up to her to decide the moral. The test might nudge her in the right direction, but no one is going to give her the answer.

Speaking of fables, here is one to help convince your child to feel free to think and answer questions in her own words:

KAPLAN'S TEST-PREP FABLES: THE PRINCESS WHO WANTED TWO BADGERS AND CEMENT BOOTS

Everyone agreed, Princess Lori was without doubt the most beautiful and difficult person in the entire kingdom. When the king asked whose hand she wanted in marriage, Lori replied she would take the first man who came through the front castle door wearing cement boots and carrying a badger in each hand. From anyone else, this statement would have been called ridiculous, but coming from Lori it was not even the fourth most difficult request she made that day.

Lured by her beauty, many suitors tried, but all failed. These men learned the hard way that knocking on a door or turning a handle when carrying a badger is an almost impossible task, especially if you have sensitive fingers. And these men were better than most, who got shinsplints from wearing cement boots and never even made it out of the construction area.

But one day Umbagog the Woodsman came to the castle. A fierce man, Umbagog was so tough he normally cut down trees just by staring at them until they fell over in fright. Umbagog showed up outside the castle wearing cement boots with steel-girder laces while holding two of the biggest, meanest badgers anyone had ever seen. He took one look at the door and then slammed his head against it, shattering it in one blow. Umbagog then married Princess Lori, and they both lived happily ever after for reasons no one could ever quite explain.

Moral: In tough situations, don't be afraid to use your head.

Session 3 is much like Session 2, although it tests both Literary Response and Expression as well as Critical Analysis and Evaluation. This means that your child will be asked to come to her own conclusions and deduce information from the text, just as she did in

Session 2. However, there will also be one essay (usually the extended-answer essay) that will ask your child to form an opinion about an issue. Often this essay will ask a question, like "Should there be a law preventing brown foxes from jumping over lazy dogs?" It is important to explain to your child that:

There is no right or wrong answer, only well-written responses versus poorly written responses.

It does not matter which side of the issue your child believes is better. All she needs to do is use proper English and support herself using facts from the passage.

We will discuss each session in greater detail throughout the rest of this chapter, but it is important to understand what skills the New York State Education Department is hoping to test with its fourth-grade English exam. If your child can tailor her attitude to fit each of the different test sessions, her overall score will benefit.

Session 1: A Day of Passages and Multiple Choices

For most students, Session 1 is going to be the session they feel the most comfortable working on, simply because reading a passage and then answering questions is probably something they have done before. As for the nature of the passages, it's a bit too soon to make many generalizations. Not enough tests have been given in the new format to say they follow any particular trend. In general, though, they are around five hundred words in length and cover topics suitable to their nine-year-old audience. Many of them are culled from existing sources, such as *Cricket* and *Jack and Jill* magazines, which contain amusing, educational, and generally positive stories. If you want to give your child more practice at reading material similar to what will appear on the English test—thus lessening his fear of the unknown—then you should:

Go to a bookstore or library and start reading children's magazines with your child.

This will help on many levels. It will give your child more exposure to reading testlike passages, it should aid in his understanding of such passages (provided you help him with positive guidance), and it should improve your child's overall reading ability. And, as if that weren't enough, it's also quality time!

Difficult words in the reading passages often have definitions in the footnotes, so make sure your child is comfortable with the footnote concept. As for themes, the passages tend more toward fiction than nonfiction, with folktales being a popular theme. However, again, not enough fourth-grade tests have been given to reveal any deeper pattern, so have your child prepared for a wide variety of formats.

While the passages may vary, the questions themselves will generally fall into four main types.

Word meanings   Supporting ideas

Summarization   Inferences and generalizations

Before we can start discussing each question type, we will need a reference passage, such as the sample that follows.

Dashiell Learns a Lesson

There once was a young ant named Dashiell who loved to play all the time. Dashiell enjoyed spending time playing with his friends more than anything else in the world.

It was fall, and time for all the ants in the meadow to trek[1] to their winter anthill in the forest. Most of the ants were busy moving their possessions because they did not want to get caught in the meadow when the cold weather and snow came. Dashiell started to move some of his items, but then the weather was so nice that Dashiell decided to take a break and enjoy the sun for a while.

"Boing, boing" sounded through the meadow. Dashiell watched as Rebecca Rabbit hopped up next to him.

"Where are you going?" asked Dashiell.

"I'm enjoying the day by hopping back and forth across the meadow. It's fun, would you like to join me?" asked Rebecca.

"Hopping seems like a lot of fun," thought Dashiell. He raised up on his hind legs and tried jumping like Rebecca did, but soon fell over on his face. When he looked up, he saw Aunt Dawn had walked up beside him.

"You still need to move your possessions to the winter anthill," said Aunt Dawn. "There's no better time than the present." Then Aunt Dawn crawled away toward the winter anthill.

Dashiell was about to go back to work, but then he saw Sylvester Snake pass near-by. "That looks like a fun way to travel," he thought. Dashiell laid his body on the ground and tried to slither like the snake did. He twisted his body on the ground for some time, but never made any progress. He stopped once his stomach started to get sore. Aunt Dawn saw Dashiell on her way back to her anthill and said, "All your belongings still need to be moved from the summer anthill. There's no better time than the present."

"Aunt Dawn is right. I should stop playing." Dashiell walked through the meadow. He heard the flutter[2] of wings above his head. Dashiell looked up to see Carol Crow flying around in the air above him.

"What are you doing?" asked Dashiell.

"I'm flying around in search of food," replied Carol Crow, who snatched a tasty grasshopper out of the air.

"Flying seems like fun. Will you help me try to fly?" asked Dashiell. He climbed up a nearby rock until he reached the top. Then he jumped off while waving his legs. Dashiell fell to the ground on his face. "Yipes," he cried, rubbing his head. Dashiell looked up and saw Aunt Dawn standing beside him.

---

1. walk or travel a great distance.
2. flapping.

"You still need to move all your belongings. There's no better time than the present." Aunt Dawn left to get more of her possessions and shook her head. "Will Dashiell ever figure it out?" she wondered.

As the sun set that day Dashiell finally got tired of playing. "Time to get to work," he said. He went to the summer anthill and picked up some of his possessions. Just then a huge rainstorm broke out. Dashiell was unable to leave the summer anthill and had to spend the night in the cold, wet anthill all by himself.

The next morning at the winter anthill Aunt Dawn awoke and saw Dashiell crawling inside with a load of his clothing. "I thought you were going to play all day again," said Aunt Dawn.

Dashiell placed the pieces of clothing down and replied, "I need to move all my belongings here. There's no better time than the present."

Aunt Dawn laughed. "I'm glad you learned that lesson, Dashiell. Put that clothing away, and then let's go get more of your possessions to move to our winter anthill."

Dashiell Learned His Lesson: Now It's Your Turn

While reading through this passage, your child should be thinking about finding the main idea. What is the whole story about? Having a main idea helps shape the entire story, giving it meaning, which should hopefully help your child in his understanding. However, while learning the main idea is important, *memorizing* the main idea is not something your child needs to do. The passage is not going anywhere after your child reads it. It stays right there for easy reference. Teach your child to:

Read to understand, not to memorize.

Once your child understands the action of the story, then it's time to start answering the questions. Children sometimes try to read the story and then answer the questions without looking back into the

LOOKING FOR MAIN IDEAS EVERYWHERE

If your child is unclear on what finding the main idea means, ask him simply to tell you a story about something that happened to him at school today. Since almost every story should have a point, when your child finishes his story, ask him what was the most important thing about what he just said. Another way to phrase this is, "If you had to retell the point of the story again in only one sentence, what would that sentence be?" The most important thing should be the main idea. Looking at a newspaper and discussing how headlines capture the main idea of a news story is another way to talk about the main idea. You can then read the story and come up with your own headlines. One exception: stay away from articles dealing with intricate, high-level finance unless you want your child's head to explode. By the way, if your child likes headlines, you can always play "Night of the Headlines!"—where one night everyone speaks only in catchy, single sentences, such as "Child Heads for Bathroom!" or "Argument over TV Remote Leads to Conflict, Then Grounding."

passage for help. If your child does this, events could get jumbled together, and this will only lead to incorrect answers. Tell your child that Session 1 of the English test is just like an open-book test. The passage is there for her to reference, so teach her to feel comfortable going back to the passage to help her answer questions correctly.

Question Type 1: Word Meanings

While some of the difficult words in the passage will have explanatory footnotes, other words will have questions devoted to them, asking your child "What does _____ mean?" It is then up to your child to figure out the meaning of the word by looking at the context, or how the word is used in the passage. Reading or hearing words in context is actually a good way for children to learn new vocabulary. It should be stressed that these are supposed to be new words, so your child should not be bothered if a word is foreign to him.

To help your child sharpen his ability to understand words in context, have him focus on the meaning of the entire sentence in which the word appears. Remember, on a multiple-choice test the answer is already there, so your child just needs a pretty good idea of what the word might mean to tell which answers are incorrect. Sometimes the meaning of the word can be gleaned from the sentence it is in, but if the meaning is not there, then either the sentence before or the sentence after will contain the necessary clues. Your child should never have to look any further than that: this is a fourth-grade test, after all. As your child looks over these sentences, have him circle any clue words that he feels help him understand the meaning of the word. In other words:

Read the words around the unknown word.

After he does this, he should be able to answer a question like the one below.

1. In the story, Dashiell thinks it would be fun to slither like Sylvester Snake. What does *slither* mean?

    A. slide

    B. fly

    C. hop

    D. crawl

Hopefully, your child chose answer A, "slide." As you can see, word-meaning questions do not ask students to give the dictionary definition of *slither*, just to choose the word that is synonymous with its meaning. When you ask your kid which words led her to that answer, she should say the words *like the snake did* and the phrase *twisted his body on the ground.*

THE MACKINUTE GAME

A fun way to help your child learn about context is to play the Mackinute game. Take turns with your child substituting the word *Mackinute* into a regular sentence: the other player has to guess what the word *Mackinute* means in that sentence. For instance, you might say, "I like my hamburgers with pickles, lettuce, tomato, and plenty of Mackinute." If your child answers "ketchup" or "mustard" or some other likely answer, ask him to pick out the words that helped him figure out the definition of the word. Try to make the game as silly as possible. Good luck, and may the best person Mackinute.

If your child prefers, tell her to look over the questions before reading each passage, and see if there are any word-meaning questions for that passage. If there are, your child should pay close attention to the italicized word in question when she reads the passage, in the hopes of understanding its meaning right away. This may help her feel more empowered about the test, but if it makes her lose track of the overall story line, it's not worth doing. In that case, just have her read the entire story and then be prepared to go back to where the word is in the passage.

THE MACKiNUTE GAME, VERSiON 2

In this variation of the Mackinute game, the rules are the same as before (see page 18), but the person now has to identify which words acted as clues in the sentence. So, when player one says, "I left the Mackinute in the oven too long and burnt its crust," player two now has to say which words (*oven, crust*) led him to guess that the Mackinute was a "pie."

Let's try another.

2. Dashiell raises up on his hind legs in the story.
What does *hind* mean?
   A. rear
   B. above
   C. top
   D. front

The sentence with the word *hind* in it contains clues like *raised up on* and *fell over on his face*, which might be enough for your child to figure out that *hind* must mean "back" or "rear." However, the sentence before also contains a clue, since Dashiell is discussing "hopping," an activity that every creature on the planet usually does with its back limbs, whatever they might be.

Question Type 2: Supporting Ideas
Plainly speaking, supporting-idea questions test how well students have read and understood small pieces of the passage. These questions are not about the "main idea." They are about the little details that, combined, make up the whole of the passage. For example, say you told your child the following story:

> A clown in a blue suit walks into a bank with a large duck on his head. The clown goes up to a teller, who asks, "Is it hard to keep that thing balanced like that?"
>
> "Not really," replied the duck. "I've got sticky webbed feet."

The supporting-idea questions would be things like "What color suit was the clown wearing?" or "What size was the duck?" These questions ask your child small facts about the passage that he is not likely to remember. If he tries to approach this Reading section the way he takes most tests (i.e., by answering questions from memory to test his knowledge), these supporting-idea queries are going to trip him up. Therefore, when looking at the English test booklet it is important to keep in mind that:

The answers to all supporting-idea questions are waiting for you in the passage.

Your child shouldn't try to trust his memory on Session 1 of the English test. Remind him that Session 1 is an "open-book" test, and using the passage is the best way to get these questions right. From memory, can either you or your child remember "Which is the first animal that Dashiell plays with?" Even if you think you can, it is smart to refer to the passage to answer this question:

3. Which is the first character that Dashiell plays with?
   A. Carol Crow
   B. Aunt Dawn
   C. Rebecca Rabbit
   D. Sylvester Snake

Looking back into the passage, your child should be able to pick C or eliminate A, B, and D, leaving C to pick. Either way, it's the correct response.

Here is another questiion:

4. Which character in the story says over and over, "There's no better time than the present."
   A. Carol Crow
   B. Aunt Dawn
   C. Rebecca Rabbit
   D. Dashiell

If your child decides not to look back at the passage, he might carelessly pick D. And he would be wrong! A review of the passage would lead him to the correct response, B.

Knowing where to look takes some understanding of the passage, but with practice your child should get better at reading a passage for its main idea while keeping a general idea of what events occurred when. Then answering supporting-idea questions becomes simply a matter of heading to a particular paragraph, reviewing the information, and answering correctly.

Question Type 3: Summarization

There will undoubtedly be questions throughout the multiple-choice section that ask, "Hey, what's the big idea?" More specifically, these questions want to know, "Hey, what's the main idea of this particular story?" Your child can learn to recognize these questions fairly easily, as the majority of them are written using phrases like "This story is mostly about _____," "What is this story mostly about?" and "What's the main idea of this story?"

Recognizing what kind of question is being asked is important, since the question type determines what strategies your child should use to answer it. In this case, knowing that a particular question is a summarization question is vital, since it means that the answer is *not* stated specifically in the passage. Your child could reread the passage forever and still not find the answer. That's why you should explain that:

HOW WATCHING TV CAN HELP IMPROVE YOUR CHILD'S SCORE

Granted, there's a catch: it has to be educational television. But if your child enjoys watching nature shows, one way to practice summarization is to ask your child to summarize sections of these shows in her own words. Nature shows, on channels ranging from Discovery to PBS, are almost always broken down into segments, like "Here's how the meerkats defend their territory" or "Two rams fight to see who's the toughest ram in the herd" or "Here a pack of hyenas go to the automated teller machine to get some money for the baseball doubleheader." This game can be played with other shows, but nature shows are a good place to start, since the segments often have a general point, yet one that is never stated outright by the narrator, who is often spending all his time trying to sound majestic.

To answer the "mostly about" questions, get the Big Picture.

Your child will have to glean a general idea of what the Reading section is about, then use the process of elimination when reviewing the answer choices. Having a general idea of the meaning of the passage helps students separate the right answer from the wrong choices, which is another reason why working on finding the main idea with your child is such a useful technique. The wrong choices are often actual facts from the passage, so they can be appealing options. But remind your child that just because a piece of information appears in the passage doesn't make it the *main* idea. A good way to think about it—and if your child can understand this, she's on her way to a successful career as a standardized-test-taker—is that wrong answers on summarization questions are often the right answer on supporting-ideas questions, and vice versa. Get it?

Think about the Dashiell passage, and what the point of the story was, then attempt the question below.

5. What is this story mostly about?
   A. Dashiell learned not to put off work until later if it could be done today.
   B. A rabbit, a snake, and a crow all played with Dashiell in the meadow.
   C. Dashiell carried his belongings from the summer anthill to the winter anthill.
   D. A crow flew nearby Dashiell, caught a grasshopper, and then flew away.

While B, C, and D are all factual, none of them encapsulate the main point of the story, which is A.

Question Type 4: Inferences and Generalizations

Inference questions, as you might expect, compel the student to infer an answer not stated specifically in the passage. Sometimes the questions will have a phrase like "will most likely" in them, showing that the answer is not 100 percent definite, only very likely definite. Like summarization questions, inference questions force the student to understand the passage and make deductions from it. For example, after the passage

> Sheryl was sick, but her brother Tommy, who was in grade school, felt fine. Sheryl's three best friends in high school were Angela, Tammy, and Brenda. Brenda lived next door, while Angela and Tammy lived across town.

an inference question would be

Since Sheryl is sick, who will probably take her homework to school for her?
   A. Tommy
   B. Angela
   C. Tammy
   D. Brenda

While this example may seem a little arbitrary (what if Tommy's grade school was next door to Sheryl's high school? What if Brenda went to a private school?), the question does contains the phrase *will probably*, which goes to show you that NYSED (New York State Education Department) knows the meaning of CYA.

What Kind of Question Is That?

Knowing the differences between the four question types helps you figure out how to approach each question. To work with your child and help him distinguish all types, discuss the difference between Question Types 1 and 2, which require specific information from the passage, and Question Types 3 and 4, which require your child to interpret information from the passage.

From the Dashiell passage, an inference question might look like

> In the passage, Aunt Dawn kept telling Dashiell "there's no better time than the present" over and over because she—
>
> A. wanted him to forget his chores and play all the time
>
> B. wanted him to stop delaying the important work he needed to do
>
> C. needed help moving her belongings
>
> D. wanted him to be the first ant to move into the winter anthill
>
> E. is working for the top-secret government shadow agency intent on helping aliens colonize Earth that can only be stopped by two hardworking FBI agents

Nowhere in the passage does it explicitly state Aunt Dawn's reason for constantly telling Dashiell, "There's no better time than the present." It is up to your child to deduce from the passage that Aunt Dawn tells Dashiell that because she "wanted him to stop delaying the important work he needed to do," answer B.

Process of elimination can also be used on the above question, and not just on answer E, the "*X-Files* trap," which commonly causes New Yorkers named Mulder and Scully to perform poorly on this section. It is important for your child to realize that these passages are written at the fourth-grade level, and when it comes to emotions:

Good feelings beat bad feelings most of the time.

The reading passages are not written by bitter, impoverished authors angry at the world. They are written by former educators, and because of this there are no depressing stories about gambling addiction or people fighting and dying in a senseless war. So if you have an inference question asking how a teacher feels, you can always cross out answers like "angry," "hateful," or "moronic," and if you have a question about why an Aunt Dawn is acting a certain way toward her nephew, you can bet that the reasons are going to be positive ones. Aunt Dawn, then, is not going to believe choice A, which is negative, or at least not very responsible of her. The best answer is B, as it is just the sort of positive, character-building answer that former educators writing the test would want children to learn.

The Funky Question and/or Passage

No, the "funky question" is not a new dance move that's all the rage with the kids. Rather, all New York parents and students should remember that since these Elementary Level tests are quite new (the first test with scores that counted was given in 1999), there will probably still be some experimenting with style and format before the test structure becomes finalized. After four or five iterations, standardized tests tend to fall into a predictable pattern. Until then, young test-takers are likely to encounter "funky"—that is, experimental or unusual—questions or passages. These passages and questions typically lower scores because students get put off and confused by the weirdness of the question format and can't seem to figure out what is expected of them.

The point is, tell your child not to worry if he comes across anything unusual. Tell him that if he encounters a strange question, he should spend some time figuring out what the question is really asking for before answering it. If he just keeps his cool, he will be ahead of the game. A funky question might look something like this:

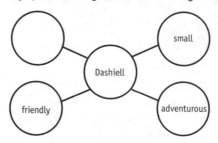

Which word would best fit into Circle 1?

    A.   speedy

    B.   playful

    C.   old

    D.   wise

Really, this question is only asking your child to pick one word that best describes Dashiell, but it does so in a somewhat unusual manner. If your child has never seen this type of question format before, he might get rattled. However, if he simply takes some time to realize that it is just an inference question asking him to pick the word that best describes Dashiell, he should find B, the correct answer.

Session 2: The Session of Listening and Writing

Session 2 is broken down into two parts:

    Part 1: Listen to a passage, then answer with 2 short responses and 1 extended response, 30 minutes.

    Part 2: Write a composition, 30 minutes.

Here is the first general point you need to emphasize to your child about Session 2:

Session 2 is not Session 1.

Seems fairly obvious, doesn't it? But the change is much more than just the different format, although that by itself is fairly momentous. Gone are the reading passages. Gone are the multiple-choice questions. Gone, in fact, are any words on paper at all, since the first part of Session 2 requires students to listen to a story and then write about it. And the most striking change between the two sessions is the one your child is least likely to notice, and that concerns what is being tested. Session 1 tests to see how well your child understands a passage, while Session 2 tests how well your child can write down her thoughts about what she has just heard.

Make sure your child takes off her multiple-choice hat and puts on her writing cap, because putting down a lot of words is one of the keys to performing well on Session 2. This is not to say that writing down just anything is effective, either—your child cannot filibuster her way to a higher score. Instead, being prepared to write down a lot is important because being afraid to write *anything* is a certain recipe for disaster. On Session 2, then, explain to your child that almost every question asked on the test is going to ask for an answer "in your own words."

The second general point your child must remember is that pacing continues to be important during Session 2. It is easy to lose track of time when writing an essay. You start worrying over exactly how to phrase something, and pretty soon the time is up—and the test is only half complete. Don't let this happen to your child. Tell her to:

Set a pace and watch her watch.

> # HOW WATCHING TV CAN HELP IMPROVE YOUR CHILD'S SCORE, PART 2
>
> It is still educational television, but if your child enjoyed watching nature shows and then searching for the main idea, then this game can be modified for the listening portion of the test simply by having your child not face the screen. Tell your child that this is the advanced version of the game. Can they still find the main idea only by listening to the announcer's words? To a generation raised on video games, the concept of the next level being more difficult should not be hard to explain, and the idea of watching TV but at the same time *not* watching TV should appeal to the perverse streak that is lurking in all nine-year-olds.

Of course, this means you will need to give your child a watch to wear (or make sure there is a clock in her classroom) and be certain she knows how to read it. The teacher administering the test will not be calling out the time except to announce when only ten minutes are remaining, so it is up to your child to keep herself on pace. Refer to the chart below for pacing suggestions:

Question	Time to Spend	Sentences in Your Answer
Part 1 (30 minutes)		
2 short responses	7 minutes/response	2–6 sentences
1 extended response	5 minutes planning, 10 minutes writing and checking over	6–10 sentences
Part 2 (30 minutes)		
1 composition	5 minutes planning, 20 minutes writing, 5 minutes checking	2 pages of text

Here is how Session 2 will start. A teacher will read a short passage to the students twice. This passage has usually been a folktale consisting of two hundred to seven hundred words. The students are instructed only to listen to the folktale the first time, but when the teacher repeats the story, the students are allowed to take notes on a page of the test. The students can then use these notes to answer the questions about the story. Some of the essay questions will deal with the main idea of the story, and some of the questions will ask students to prove a point using examples from the story.

This means that when your child listens to the story for the second time, she will be instructed to write down parts of the story to use as examples. And since some of the questions will ask about the main idea of the story, tell your child:

The first time through, listen for the main idea. The second time through, listen for examples that support the main idea.

After the second reading, your child needs to have a rough idea of what he thinks the story is about as well as some notes from the story to back up his theory. Mix in a willingness to write, then add a pinch of correct grammar, and your child is ready to take on some essay questions. Before we approach the questions, however, let's take a look at a sample passage, "The Mongoose Brothers and the Cotton Shirt." This story, of course, has been a classic bedtime favorite with children since 1999. Read this story to your child twice.

The Mongoose Brothers and the Cotton Shirt

There were once two mongoose brothers who were each given a bag of seeds from their father. "I will give away my farm to the brother who makes the most out of his bag of seeds," said the father.

"Oh, I am going to win!" exclaimed the older brother. "I will get an automobile out of these seeds!"

"And I will try to make a shirt," said the younger brother.

"Then you will definitely lose," said the older brother, "because an automobile easily beats a shirt!"

The older brother went off to find someone who would trade his car for a bag of seeds, while the younger brother went outside and planted the seeds from his bag. After three months several large cotton plants had grown. The younger brother picked the cotton and wove a simple, short-sleeved shirt out of it.

When the father returned, the younger brother gave his father the shirt. The older brother still had his bag of seeds, since he was unable to find anyone who would trade his car for the seeds. The father gave the farm to the younger brother and said, "A real shirt beats a make-believe car every time."

After hearing this story for the first time, your child should have formed some understanding of the main idea, which could be described as "the younger brother wins the farm because he makes something out of the seeds, while the older brother talks a big game but gets nothing done." Granted, that is a long main idea, but hopefully your child will have at least a part of that idea after the first reading. A shorter version is "something beats nothing." While both versions are right, the longer version does show a greater understanding of the events in the story.

On the second reading, your child should write down the key facts, such as what the older brother tries to do with his bag of seeds versus what the younger brother does. These notes do not have to be verbatim, so do not stress out your child by asking her to learn shorthand. However, your child does need to able to refer to the facts of the story correctly. She cannot talk about how the younger brother planted corn or flax, since that would be wrong. It was cotton. This is what is meant by a *key fact*. Your child does not have to write down exactly what father mongoose says at the end, but she has to write down why the father mongoose awarded the farm to the younger brother.

The Long and the Short of Short-Response Questions

Now, on to the questions. The two short-response questions are similar to inference questions in Session 1, in the sense that the student is given a quotation from the story and then asked to infer its meaning. Sample questions might be something like

1. In the beginning of the story, the older brother says, "You will certainly lose." Why does he believe that?

    or

2. Look at the following quotation, then give its meaning in the story. "A real shirt beats a make-believe car every time."

    or

3. In your own words, explain why the father awards the farm to the younger brother. Use details from the story in your answer.

For all of these questions, a long one-sentence answer might suffice, but in general it would be easier to answer all of them with about two sentences. The last short response, though, asks for details, so it might take three or four sentences. Remember, your child has about seven minutes to answer each of these questions. There is no need to rush, but there is also no time to dawdle. Correct answers will include key facts from the story.

Extended-Response Questions

After the two short response questions, there is a "planning page" for the extended-response question. Your child should read that question, then spend about five minutes planning how she wants to respond. For example, the extended-response question might be something like this:

Which moral does this story teach best?

Something is always better than nothing.

Actions speak louder than words.

Circle one, then explain how the story
teaches that moral. Use examples from
the folktale in your answer.

The first pitfall a student might fall into on the extended-response question is the mistaken belief that one of these morals is wrong, and the other moral is right. This would be true if this were a Session 1 question, but the student is now in Session 2, where what matters is how well the child can express herself. Your child must remember:

If you can support your answer with examples from the story, then it is right.

After spending about five minutes planning her response, your child should write out her answer neatly (graders cannot grade what they cannot read) in ten minutes or so, being sure to keep some time at the end to look over her work and correct any spelling and grammar errors as well as to add any words she might have omitted the first time by mistake.

Part 2: The Composition
Sounds like the title of a horror movie, doesn't it? For children who do not like to write a lot, this coincidence is a little too accurate to be amusing. Yet there is one positive note about this thirty-minute essay:

All the facts your child needs to write the composition are already in her head.

No more reading passages to refer back to, no more listening to stories and then jotting down key facts. The composition is testing one thing, pure and simple: What kind of an essay writer is your child? Realize that your son or daughter could become the greatest fiction writer ever to walk this planet and still have troubles with the essay form. For the essay, organization and detail are the two key elements that can transform a muddled, rambling essay into a sharp, well-worded composition.

Here is a sample composition question:

Write about a time when someone you know showed you
how to do something for the first time. Or, write about
a time you showed someone how to do something for
the first time. Be sure to include

what exactly was taught

who taught the lesson

what occurred afterward

specific details and examples

With thirty minutes to write this essay, your child need not start wildly jotting down the first idea that comes into his head. Rather, the key to the whole composition is in the first five minutes, when your child uses the planning page (one is provided for the composition as well) to sketch out the outline of what he wants to say and what details he is going to use to back up his essay. And the more specific, the better. Look at the sample first sentences below, and see how each one gets more specific and should therefore lead to a clearer, better composition.

> This is a story about how I built a car.

> This is a story about how I built my first soapbox car.

> This is a story about how I built my first soapbox car with the help of my dad.

> I remember clearly the morning I built my first soapbox car with my father's help: the morning was cold, chilly, as if the night was still battling the sun for possession of the Earth, fighting to keep its spectral, frosty hands wrapped around our fragile planet.

These four examples could be graded Poor, Adequate, Good, and Very Good but a Little Melodramatic.

If your child has spent the proper time planning and writing a tidy three-paragraph essay, do not worry if it only takes him fifteen minutes to write. Your child should not tack something more on the end to increase the word count. Since the essay should be as specific and detailed as needed, any time remaining at the end should once again be spent reading over the work for spelling and grammar errors. If your child finishes either the extended-response question or the composition without giving himself time to look over his work, he is doing himself a great disservice. If he has extra time after looking over the composition, have him review the rest of his writing in the section. Make sure your child spends the entire sixty minutes of Session 2 working on his writing skills. When the teacher tells everyone to stop, he can place his pencil down triumphantly on the desk and say, "Two sessions down, one to go."

Session 3: Last Day of the English Language Arts Test

Sometimes math is helpful on the English exam. Everyone knows that $1 + 2 = 3$, and on the New York State fourth-grade tests, Session 1 + Session 2 = Session 3. Session 3 takes reading passages like the students saw in Session 1 and then asks them to write short-response answers about them like they did in Session 2.

Pacing for Session 3

Read the first passage	5 minutes
Answer 2 short responses	10 minutes
Read second passage and answer 1 short response	10 minutes
Review 3 short-response answers	5 minutes
Plan extended response	5 minutes
Write extended response	20 minutes
Check work	5 minutes

The last day of testing starts off with a long reading passage, such as a six-hundred-word nonfiction passage. This passage is followed by two short-response questions similar to the questions asked after the listening passage in Session 2. After these two questions, there is a shorter reading passage on a subject related to the first passage, followed by one short-response question on that passage. For instance, if the first passage talks about centipedes, then the second passage would be about the differences between centipedes and millipedes. The three short-response questions will test your child on how well she understands and can write about each passage in her own words. To do well on these questions, your child must remember that this section is like an open-book test (as it was in Session 1), but that the answers need to be in short-response form (as they were in Session 2).

The short-response questions should take about half of the testing period, or about thirty minutes.

The last half of this exam day is where Session 3 differs from the previous two sessions. As you may recall from the beginning of this chapter, this exam day is supposed to test how well your child can analyze information and come up with a conclusion. This means that the extended-response essay in Session 3 will ask your child to do two main things:

1. *Use information from both reading passages.*
2. *Make some conclusions and support them with details.*

The extended-response question might ask, "Explain whether you would prefer to have centipedes or millipedes living in your backyard." It does not matter whether your child chooses centipedes or millipedes, it only matters that she picks one of the little critters, and then writes convincingly about why she prefers that insect over the other insect, making sure to use facts from both of the passages.

Since your child is allowed to flip around through the different pages in this section of the test, make sure she refers back to the passages whenever necessary, which means basically after every question. Why trust memory for a key fact when the source is readily available? During the essay planning stage, when your child is gathering key facts and details to support her main idea/topic sentence in the essay, she should be flipping the pages between the two passages and the planning page repeatedly.

In a way, how well your child handles Session 3 depends on how well she utilized the different techniques in Sessions 1 and 2. If she always referred back to the passage for the multiple-choice questions, then referring back to the passages to answer the short-answer and extended-response questions should be second nature. And if your child became comfortable with the idea of writing down answers to open-ended questions in her words (supported, of course, by facts from the passages), then nothing in Session 3 should cause her any great difficulty.

Chapter Three MATHEMATICS

How the Math Test Adds Up

Like its English Language Arts sibling, the Mathematics exam is taken in three sessions, each with its own day.

Day 1	30 multiple-choice questions	40 minutes
Day 2	9 open-ended questions (7 short, 2 extended)	50 minutes
Day 3	9 open-ended questions (7 short, 2 extended)	50 minutes

Once again, New York fourth-graders are given one day of multiple-choice before facing two more days of broader, open-ended questions. The short, open-ended questions count for up to two points each, while the extended open-ended questions count for up to three points each. Assuming that the multiple-choice questions count for one point each, a perfect score on the Math section would add up to seventy points: thirty on the first day and twenty on each subsequent day.

This means that although there are twice as many days of open-ended questions, the first day of multiple-choice questions accounts for a greater percentage of a student's overall score than any other day. Since about 43 percent of all possible points are available on the first day of testing, make sure to tell your child:

> *Compared with the other two days, the first day of testing counts the most toward your score, and this is good news because test-taking strategies are most effective against the multiple-choice format.*

You do not want your child getting an ulcer, worried that a bad first day will scuttle his score. What you want your child to understand is that almost half of all the math answers will be sitting in front of him in Session 1. All he has to do is pick out the correct answer or eliminate any incorrect answers and then take a guess.

An Open-Ended Discussion about Open-Ended Questions

Some of these questions are worth up to two points, while others are worth up to three. There is no clear distinction between the two questions, no large sign that says "Three-point question here!" However, the last question on both Sessions 2 and 3 has usually been worth three points, with the other three-point question lurking near the end of both sections.

While the multiple-choice part of the exam is scored by a machine, the two- and three-point questions are scored by New York teachers who have been given guidelines about what constitutes a three-point answer, a two-point response, a one-point response, and no points at all. For the two-pointers, to get full credit your child has to respond in a manner that is "complete and correct," meaning that not only is the correct answer visible, but that adequate work is shown to demonstrate your child arrived at the answer by using her math skills and not her powerful psychic ability.* If your child has the correct answer, but without any explanation, that is only worth one point. And the reverse is also worth one point: incorrect answer, but with a "mathematically appropriate process." So, as we stated in chapter 1, remind your child that on every open-ended question

Show your work, and give every question your best shot using sound math skills.

The following little fable might help convince your child of the importance of this strategy:

Pace Yourself

Here are some guidelines to tell your child about how long he should spend on each question per session.

Day 1: Roughly one minute per question. Since there is only a ten-minute cushion (thirty questions, forty minutes), remind your child never to get bogged down on any question. A good rule of thumb on a tough question is to spend a minute working on it, then take an educated guess and move on.

Days 2 & 3: Five minutes per question. Your child might wish to do a two-pass system on these sections, going through the first time answering any questions that seem fairly easy. This should give him additional time on the harder problems, but it is not a good idea to have a child work more than ten minutes on any one question. It would get too frustrating and may hurt his confidence.

---

*If your child does have such psychic abilities, tell her to concentrate her mental efforts on the multiple-choice section, since you do not have to show any work on those questions.

KAPLAN'S TEST-PREP FABLES:
THADDEUS THE ARTIST AND
THE 51 PERCENT FIRING SQUAD

One day in the kingdom of Schmooland, the king's loyal attendants were dusting the king's favorite painting of himself when they made an unwelcome discovery. Some villainous knave had painted a tacky mustache and ridiculous horns on the royal portrait! The whole kingdom went into an uproar, and the king demanded that all subjects search for the person responsible. Eventually, many Schmoolandians started to whisper that Thaddeus the Artist was the person who had made the unflattering additions to the painting. These people had no evidence, but were jealous of Thaddeus and his hip, downtown lifestyle that included lots of coffee drinking, black turtlenecks, and incense.

In a rage, the king wanted justice, and although there was no real evidence, a judge declared Thaddeus guilty and ordered him executed.

"But, Judge," replied Thaddeus, "since there's no actual proof that I committed this crime, isn't it unfair to say that I'm one hundred percent guilty? Isn't it more like I'm fifty-one percent guilty, and forty-nine percent innocent?" The judge pondered this statement and, realizing that his judgment was only given because the king was angry, decided that Thaddeus was indeed only 51 percent guilty.

The day of the execution arrived, and Thaddeus was placed before the firing squad. When asked if he had a final request, Thaddeus said, "Since I am only fifty-one percent guilty, I should only be fifty-one percent executed." The officer in charge of the firing squad agreed and ordered his men to use only 51 percent of the usual gunpowder. When fired, the weakened bullets bounced off the artist's stiff smock, which was covered in dried paint and shellac. The officer in charge decided he had done his job, and let Thaddeus go.

A free man, Thaddeus found the real culprit, and then he wrote a screenplay about his exploits, which was made into a movie starring Harrison Ford that did tremendously well at the box office.

Moral #1: Partial credit can make a big difference.

Moral #2: Harrison Ford is a big-time box-office draw.

On the three-point questions, you can earn up to two points even if you have an incorrect answer.

All this talk about partial credit is not meant to encourage your child to not worry about getting the right answer. He should not answer the question "What is 7 minus 2?" with the response "Something around 3." The whole purpose of the discussion is to make sure your child does not freeze up when he encounters a difficult-looking open-ended question.

Free Stuff! Free Stuff!

If you consider the Math exam as a three-day journey, then the three types of items NYSED gives to your child would be the provisions. Every New York fourth-grader taking this test is given items described as Punch-Out Tools. The Punch-Out Tools are a ruler, counters, and pattern blocks. A sample of each appears in the back of the book.

The ruler measures both metric and standard lengths. There are fourteen counters, and six different geometric shapes (hexagon, triangle, trapezoid, square, and two rhomboids). Although these make swell stocking stuffers any time of the year, they are actually given out for a purpose. Your child will be called upon to use each of these items at some point in the test, perhaps in a question like this:

Use your pattern blocks to solve this problem.

Michael created the design below using his pattern blocks.

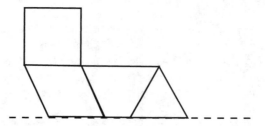

Complete the design below so that the dotted line is a line of symmetry. Trace around your pattern blocks to show the other half of the design.

The first thing your child should notice about this problem is that it starts out with the sentence "Use your pattern blocks to solve this problem." This advice is vital to answering the problem. When a ruler is needed, the statement says, "Use your ruler to solve this problem." However, when referring to the counters, the statements always read, "You *may* use your counters to help you solve this problem." The counters are not critical to solving the problems, and if your child happens to have two extra fingers on each hand, they could even be called redundant.

MAKE ME A TRAIN!

To give your child more experience with pattern blocks, cut out the shapes in this book and add a circle. Then ask your child to use the blocks and draw certain familiar shapes, such as a house or dog. You should start with simple shapes, then make the game harder as you go along. For instance, the first shape could be a car, but then the next shape is a fire engine, followed by a sports car, followed by a dune buggy. When your child can use these shapes to accurately draw a red 1964 Mustang convertible with an eight-cylinder engine, your work on this skill is done.

***When the test asks the student to use either the ruler or the
pattern blocks, those tools are critical to solving the problem.
Using the counters is not critical to solving the problem.***

Some questions involving the ruler simply ask your child to measure a drawing accurately, while others make your child measure a figure, such as a square, and then determine the area of the square. In the former question, using the ruler correctly is the entire question, while in the second example the ruler is just the first step of a two-step process.

Back to our pattern-block problem. Another thing you will notice about this problem is that there are no multiple-choice answers, meaning that this is an open-ended question. Since the problem revolves around two central issues—"Does the student know what a line of symmetry is?" and "Can the student use the pattern blocks correctly?"—the question is only a two-point question. If your child remembers that a line of symmetry means she will have to draw a mirror image of the drawing, the problem now becomes one that could use P.O.E. Which of the pattern blocks are used on the left side? If your child eliminates all the ones that are not used, the final step is to place the proper four blocks in the correct place and then trace around their edges.

What the Math Test Tests

The fourth-grade Math test is designed to test New York students in seven different skills areas. According to the New York State Education Department, these seven Learning Standards are:

Key Idea 1:   *Mathematical Reasoning (10–15% of test)*
                 Basic word problems, usually involving using addition or subtraction to figure out an unknown quantity.

Key Idea 2:   *Numbers and Numeration (15–25%)*
                 Understanding of basic math terminology such as fractions, whole numbers, and other concepts.

Key Idea 3:   *Operations (20–25%)*
                 Problem-solving using addition, subtraction, multiplication, and division.

Key Idea 4:   *Modeling/Multiple Representation (5–10%)*
                 Geometric shapes and concepts.

Key Idea 5:   *Measurement (15–20%)*
                 Graphs and charts, measuring ability, and concepts related to volume, perimeter, and circumference.

Key Idea 6:   *Uncertainty (5–10%)*

Key Idea 7:   *Patterns/Function (10–15%)*

The bulk of this chapter will cover these Key Ideas in detail, but before we begin, we need to make one more point about the fourth-grade Math exam. In general, vaguely worded questions in this section cause students a good deal of confusion. Tasks in this section are rarely as straightforward as "Divide 48 by 6," although some of these do appear, usually near the beginning of the test. Instead, the questions are often trying to see not whether students can divide, but if they know *when* is the right time to divide. To accomplish this, the above question might appear as

> There are 48 people who need to be seated at 6 differ-
> ent tables. Each table must have the same number of
> people seated there. How many people will be seated at
> each table?
>
> A. 6
>
> B. 8
>
> C. 24
>
> D. 48

Or the same question might be seen as this:

> There are 48 people who need to be seated at a restau-
> rant. The restaurant has 6 different tables. Each table
> must have the same number of people seated there. In
> the space below, draw a diagram to represent this infor-
> mation.

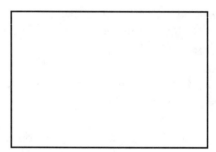

How many people are seated at each table?

All three questions pose the same math problem, but to answer questions two and three correctly the student must be able to say to himself, "Hey, this is a *division* question." (The third question, as you may have noticed, was an open-ended question worth two points.) This oblique approach to the Key Ideas is prevalent throughout the exam, which is why many intelligent kids get frustrated and wind up with a low score. They know a certain math skill, such as division, quite well, but they don't realize that the exam is often more concerned with discerning if the students know when they're supposed to use that particular math skill. Once your child gets comfortable with the NYSED approach to math, the math section gets a little easier.

Key Idea 1: Mathematical Reasoning (10–15% of test)

Math reasoning is in many ways like basic algebra in that they both often center around the question "What is the value of the missing number?" The NYSED definition of this Key Idea is "Students use mathematical reasoning to analyze mathematical situations," but whichever way you cut it, it boils down to questions that look like

You may use your counters to help you solve this problem.

Nicki has 4 baseball cards. Nicki and Larry together have 9 baseball cards. Larry and Justin together have 7 baseball cards. How many baseball cards does Justin have?

A. 9

B. 5

C. 2

D. 4

The reason this could be considered basic algebra is that the question boils down to N = 4, N + L = 9, L + J = 7. Does this mean the best way to solve this problem is to teach your child basic algebra? No, no, a thousand times no! The best way to solve this question is to have your child take the problem one step at a time. Many children who get this problem wrong do so because they try to skip Larry (the middle unknown quantity) due to time constraints and get right to Justin's baseball card stash. However, if your child takes her time and uses the counters if she wants to, she will first answer the crucial question "How many cards does Larry have?" Once she figures out that Larry has 5 cards, if Larry and Justin have 7 cards together, that means that Justin must have 2 cards, answer C. This question could be considered a simple addition/subtraction question, but it sure does not appear that obvious at first glance, now does it?

On the open-ended question side, the multistep process is the same, and the questions again center around determining the values of a missing number, or numbers.

THE CHANGE GAME, AKA PETTY BRIBERY

If you do not mind parting with small amounts of money, play the Change Game with your child. Assemble a collection of pennies, nickels, dimes, and quarters, then present various amounts of change to your child and ask her to tell you how many cents she has. If she gets the amount correct, add or subtract various pieces of currency, simulating addition or subtraction. Add or subtract the money in word form, though, asking your child questions like, "If Bob has the amount of money below, and Bob and Joanie together have a dollar thirty-five, then how much money does Joanie have?" You could also quiz your child by saying, "If the amount of money here needed to be split three ways, how much would each person have?" If your child gets three answers in a row correct, she gets to "keep the change." If your child is very bright, stay away from using Susan B. Anthonys.

In the number sentences below, the same shape always stands for the same number.

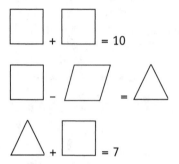

Part A

Use the number sentences to find which numbers the △, ☐, and ▱ stand for. Write the correct number in each shape above.

Part B

On the lines below, explain the steps you used to find the answer.

While this question looks much more involved than the previous baseball-card question, it is really similar. Nicki is the square, Larry is a triangle, and Justin is the rhombus. (Sorry to be the one to tell you you're a square, Nicki.) Note that if your child just answered the question with no explanation, he would not receive total credit, as Part B awaits. However, Part B does not require your child to talk about the question in math terms, saying something like "I deduced the value of the first variable, and then used this information to subsequently deduce the values of the other two variables in the third and second math equations, respectively." A sufficient answer for Part B would be "First I figured out the square was 5 since two of the same number put together equal 10. Then I filled in all the squares with 5. Then I figured out the triangle was 2, since 2 + 5 = 7, so I filled in all the triangles with 2. I knew 5 - 2 = 3, so I put a 3 in the other four-sided figure."

This sounds wordy, but this is a three-point question. Part B merely asks your child to write out what he did, step by step. This seems tough, but it can actually work to your child's advantage. Even if he only figures out the squares, and then gets lost on the triangles, that might still be good enough for partial credit if he can explain his thought process.

Key Idea 2: Numbers and Numeration (15–25%)

Numbers and numeration are two Key Ideas tested heavily in the Math section. Numbers and numeration questions test a student's knowledge and understanding of such basic math principles as whole numbers, integers, even/odd numbers, consecutive order, decimals, fractions, ratios, percents, and irrational numbers (all the basics you learned as a child but have long since forgotten). What makes these concepts difficult is how they are presented on the test. Some of the questions are straightforward, like

70 quarters   15 quarters   33 quarters   25 quarters

Which of these piggy banks has an even number of quarters?

   A. 70 quarters

   B. 15 quarters

   C. 33 quarters

   D. 25 quarters

Unless your child makes a careless error, chances are good she will get A as an answer. Other problems, however, are not so obvious.

The students at Piedmont Elementary are collecting sticks for an art project. The pictures below show the number of sticks they have collected so far.

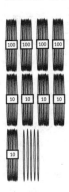 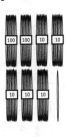

How many sticks do the students have after collecting them for three weeks?

   A. 808

   B. 880

   C. 708

   D. 826

This question covers up what it is asking fairly well. The trick is for your child not to get flustered if he does not understand what to do initially. He should ask himself, "What does this question want me to do with all these numbers?" After some calm thought, he will probably realize the answer is "Add them together."

Make sure your child is comfortable with basic math terms.

Some of the more popular terms to know are *fractions, ratios,* and *percents.* Your child can be fairly certain there will be a question or two on each of these topics, so it is important that she truly understands and feels comfortable with these subjects. A question involving these terms might look like this:

You may use your counters to help you solve this problem.

Label the donuts on the table below to show that

1/4 are glazed (G),

1/3 are chocolate (C), and

the rest are plain (P).

What fraction of the donuts on the table are plain?

On a question like the one above, just being able to recognize a fraction will not be enough to get it right. A clear understanding of how fractions work is needed. On the question above, three of the donuts should be glazed, and four are chocolate, leaving five plain. The answer to the second part of the question would then be 5/12.

Key Idea 3: Operations (20–25%)

Old-time test-takers knew these types of questions by another name: *word problems.* Your child is presented with a situation requiring her to decide whether addition, subtraction, multiplication, or division is needed to find the right answer. On the fourth-grade test, these questions sometimes appear as

6 x 86 =

PETTY BRIBERY, PART ii

To help your child work more with fractions and other basic terms, simply add these types of questions to the Bribery Game. With percents, you should start with a dollar, since 100 cents = 1 dollar, so the number of cents is always the percentage of a dollar (25 cents = 25%). Gather like groups of currency together to work on fractions. For example, you might use a group of eight dimes and ask your child, "If I had one-fourth of these dimes, how many cents would I have?" For ratios, using two different groups of change would work, such as gathering six dimes and two nickels and asking, "What is the ratio of dimes to nickels?"

A. 486

B. 4836

C. 648

D. 516

E. None of these

But do not hold your breath for too many questions this easy. At most, there will be two on the entire math test. Instead, the typical word problem will be more like

> Edward wants to practice playing his trombone for a total of 140 minutes over 4 days. Edward practices his trombone for 50 minutes on Tuesday, 35 minutes on Wednesday, and 27 minutes on Thursday. How minutes should Edward practice on Friday?
>
> *Show your work.*

To do well on word-problem questions, your child must take some time, perhaps even reread the question, and then decide which mathematical operation is needed.

> ***Figuring out whether addition, subtraction, multiplication, or division is needed is a crucial part of all word problems.***

In the trombone problem above, your child will have to realize that the four days of practice need to total 140 minutes. In fact, if your child wants to write out a mini-calendar like

Tues.	Wed.	Thurs.	Fri.
50	35	27	???

That would be a good idea, since to get two full points she would need to show her work. These numbers need to be added and then subtracted from 140 minutes to find the answer, 28 minutes. Or, your child could subtract each number from 140 and reach the answer that way as well.

THE LiBRARY GAME

This is an imaginative way to work on word-problem skills with your child. You start out with one book, and one person is the librarian, who adds to the collection, and the other person is Anti-Book Dude, who takes away from the collection. The librarian starts by saying, "I purchased one book." Anti-Book Dude must now invent a way to take away two books, such as "Two books were destroyed in a small fire." The librarian must now add three books, but he cannot use the same way as before (purchasing), so he must come up with another way, like "Three books were donated by a wealthy woman." Now it's Anti-Book Dude's turn. Try to see how high a number you and your child can reach before running out of ideas. The early version deals with only addition and subtraction, but you can play the advanced game that also uses multiplication and division, by posing problems such as "The library doubled its number of books. How many books are in the library now?" or "One-fourth of all books were eaten by locusts. How many books are left?" Hopefully, your child will gain some familiarity with the idea of which words take away and which words add, but even if that does not work, it is still quality family time.

Key Idea 4: Modeling/Multiple Representation (5–10%)

We know this Key Idea by a simpler word: *geometry*. Your child will probably be asked one graph question—the whole (x,y) coordinate grid stuff—and then two to four other questions regarding geometric principles. While you might think most of these questions would require the use of the pattern blocks, this is not actually the case. However, your child will need to know the definition of the basic shapes (square, circle, quadrilateral, triangle), and he should also feel comfortable with various geometric concepts such as lines and angles. Sometimes on the open-ended questions, your child will be required to define a geometric shape as the second part of a two-point question.

Try the following question:

How many line segments are in the figure below?

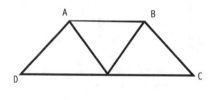

A. 3

B. 6

C. 7

D. 9

> ## SUGAR CUBE CASTLE
>
> For a time-intensive but fun way to teach your child about different geometric shapes, buy a box or two of sugar cubes, get some glue, and construct a small castle using the cubes. All the basic shapes can be created: the towers could be cylinders, the front wall a rectangle composed of cubes, and pyramids and triangles can be placed along the tower wall. To make a sphere, some careful nibbling will have to be done, but who doesn't like sugar?

If your child does not know exactly what a line is, he could still do some process of elimination and then take a guess. Since there are three triangles in the picture, answer A is a trap for students who would like to think that a line is a triangle. Hopefully, even if your child does not know what a line is, he will be familiar enough with the concept to know that a line is not a triangle. After eliminating A, he should just take a guess: a one-in-three shot isn't that bad. The answer is B.

If your child has never been a great fan of geometry, he can take comfort in that there are not many questions about it on the Math exam. If your child is a big fan of geometry, tell him that there are roughly four questions on the whole test that will be easy prey for a quadrilateral-loving fool such as him.

Key Idea 5: Measurement (15–20%)

Ladies and gentlemen, start your rulers! Measurement questions do ask students to measure various drawings accurately, but this category also includes other question types, most notably graphs and charts. In addition to these two main question types, there is usually one time-measurement question, so make sure your child can tell time using a standard watch (one with hands, not a digital display).

The measurement questions that require your child to use her ruler often ask her to perform more than just that one task. For instance, in the question

Use your ruler to help you solve this problem.

Part A

> Measure each piece of string shown below to the nearest centimeter. Write the length in the space next to each drawing.

Part B

> Only the pieces of string longer than 5 centimeters need to be saved. Circle each piece of string above that is *longer* than 5 centimeters.

Your child gets a point just if she can measure accurately, and another point if she draws circles around the first and last figures, since they are longer than five centimeters. However, measurement questions sometimes get a little trickier and ask your child about such concepts as area, volume, and perimeter. So Part B in the question above might look like this:

Part B

> The four pieces of string are then joined at the ends to form a quadrilateral. What is the perimeter, in centimeters, of this quadrilateral?

Your child may even see something like this on a three-point question:

Part C

> Each of the four strings is stretched so that each string is now 2 centimeters longer than it originally was. What is the perimeter, in centimeters, of this new quadrilateral?

GEOMETRIC-SHAPE SCAVENGER HUNT

A good way to help your child remember the names of different shapes is to have a household scavenger hunt. Get everyone looking around for items that are triangles, cubes, spheres, and so forth.

GEOMETRIC-SHAPE SCAVENGER HUNT, PART ii

You can make your scavenger hunt a little more challenging by getting more specific. Instead of just asking your child to find a square, a cube, or a sphere, arm him with a ruler and send him in search of "a rectangle with a perimeter of more than thirty inches" or "a triangle with an area of less than twelve square inches." That way, he will have to recognize and measure the shapes he finds.

To answer such a question, your child must start by measuring accurately. He must then use the measurements to find either perimeter, area, circumference, or some other dimension. Of course, this means your child has to know what words like *perimeter*, *area*, and *circumference* mean, so make sure these concepts are familiar to him.

Measurement questions involving graphs and charts can be broken down into two tidy little categories, simple and advanced.

Simple: your child must read the graph correctly.

Advanced: your child must make the graph correctly.

As you might expect, the simple graph questions are usually in the multiple-choice section, while the advanced questions are two- or three-point open-ended questions. Simple graph problems often feature multiple questions referring to the same graph, and they look like this:

FOR THOSE OF YOU SCORING AT HOME . . .

Various kinds of charts are scattered throughout every newspaper, but if you want to go to the place that charts call home, turn to the scoreboard page of the sports section. There you will always find as many charts as there were games last night. Explain to your child what the various markings mean, then ask questions like "Who had the most hits in this baseball game?" or "How many more runs did the Rangers score in the fourth inning than the Yankees?" Questions like "This bum playing shortstop went hitless and yet still got paid $400,000 for the game. Where's the justice in that?" are socially relevant, but should not be asked of your child because they rarely appear on the New York exam.

The graph below shows how many raffle tickets Ms. Diaz's class sold during one week. Study the graph, then answer the following questions.

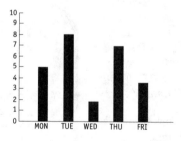

Ms. Diaz promised that the class could work on their art project on the day the total number of tickets sold reached 16. The bar graph shows the number of tickets sold each day.

What day did Ms. Diaz let the class work on their art project?

    A. Friday

    B. Thursday

    C. Wednesday

    D. Tuesday

How many days did the students sell more than 6 tickets?

    A. 2

    B. 3

    C. 4

    D. 5

In both questions, the test never just asks for information from the chart, like "How many tickets were sold on Tuesday?" In each case, your child needs to read the graph and then use the information in some manner. In the first question, this means adding the ticket sales each day until the number 16 is reached, on Thursday. The second question is essentially a P.O.E. question: Which days can be eliminated because fewer than six tickets were sold? Only two days are left, leaving answer A.

An advanced, open-ended question might look like this:

Ms. Diaz's class sold raffle tickets for one week to pay for an upcoming class trip. The results are shown below.

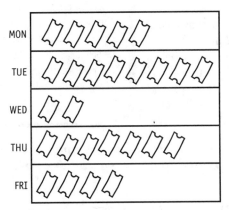

On the grid that follows, make a bar graph showing the number of raffle tickets sold each day. Use the information in the table above to help you.

Be sure to:

- title the graph
- label the axes
- graph all the data

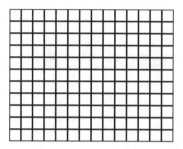

Part B

Using the information from your graph, write *one* statement comparing ticket sales.

At this point, no doubt many of you parents are feeling grateful that you do not have to take this test. Granted, this is a three-point question, and deservedly so, but it can still be completed if your child feels good about making charts. Any number of answers to part B could be correct. Graders want your child to show that he can interpret the graph he just created. A correct answer could be a statement like "There are only 2 days where the students sold more than 6 tickets" or "the students reached 16 total tickets on Thursday."

CHART YOUR VEGETABLES!

To give your child some experience making charts, you first need to buy some grid paper. Then, it's just a quick trip into your kitchen, where you can ask your child to graph all sorts of items. How many vegetables are there? How many different types of soup are there? Make sure that your child always puts numbers along the vertical line and a description of what is being graphed along the horizontal line. The rest is counting. If your child does a thorough job of graphing your food supplies, be sure to use the information on your next shopping trip. While everyone else has a shopping list, you will have a shopping grid.

For advanced graph questions on the open-ended section, be prepared to make a graph or chart.

Key Idea 6: Uncertainty (5–10%)

Although their name does not suggest it, uncertainty questions certainly fall into two major categories, estimating and probability. Estimating questions are general visual questions that ask students to eyeball a small amount and then decide how many of the small amounts will fit into a bigger amount.

This box has about 30 pennies in it.

Which of these boxes has the amount closest to 90 pennies?

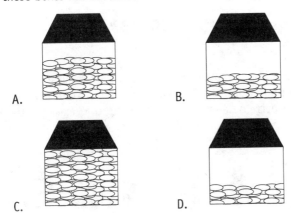

A.

B.

C.

D.

Note that on a question like this one, your child could use his ruler if he wanted to. It could certainly help your child estimate the height of ninety pennies, which should be three times the height of thirty pennies, or answer A.

Probability questions are usually rather straightforward, but that doesn't make them easy. If the concept of probability was easier to grasp, perhaps more people could quit their day jobs and make a living at casinos and racetracks. Unless your child is a bookie, she may have a little trouble. Take a look at the following question, for example:

Jake will choose one coin from the group of change above. What is the probability he will choose a dime?

A. 1/7

B. 3/7

C. 4/7

D. 10/7

As there are three dimes out of seven coins, the answer is B. Perhaps because the concept of probability is so hard, the test-makers made the questions more straightforward. Luckily, there are not many uncertainty questions on the New York exam. Don't spend too much time trying to explain the concept of probability to your child. You may frustrate and worry her unnecessarily. If she is curious, you can try using a die to explain the general principle. Show her the six sides on the die, each with a different number of dots. The probability that any side will appear when you roll the die is one in six. That's the basic idea. It is probably best to leave the discussion at that, unless you want to confuse yourself and your kid.

Key Idea 7: Patterns/Function (10–15%)

"Prepare for launch: 6, 5, 4, 3, 2 . . ."

What number comes next? If your child knows the answer to that question, she is on the path to answering pattern questions. On the New York exam, pattern questions fall into two categories: "Find the pattern" and "Add up the parts that make up the pattern." Pattern questions in the first category look like this:

Study the pattern below.

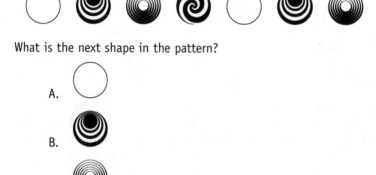

What is the next shape in the pattern?

A.

B.

C.

D.

On questions like these, tell your child to be prepared for patterns in groups of four, like the problem above. Why four? While it would be rash to say that there will always be four shapes that repeat, consider what the test designers' thought process must have been. They probably thought a pattern involving groups of two would be too easy. Since previous tests have had four shapes, we might assume the test-makers thought three shapes were too easy as well. Five is a remote possibility, but six would be extremely difficult, so four it is! Since it is a four-character pattern above, the answer is A.

On questions involving repeating patterns, first look for patterns that repeat after every four characters.

Questions that ask you to add up the parts that make up the pattern are a little tougher, and they often look like the problem below.

This staircase is 4 steps high.

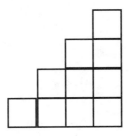

What would be the total number of squares if the staircase was 6 steps high?

    A.   10

    B.   15

    C.   21

    D.   24

To solve this type of pattern problem, *just continue the pattern and then add things up.* There are 10 squares to start with, so adding 5 squares and then 6 more would make 10 + 5 + 6 = 21. Then it's off to the answer choices! Our old friend process of elimination could help if your child got stumped on this pattern question. Clearly, if we started with 10 squares and then added more steps, choice A could not be correct. Your child can cross out this choice and then take a guess.

Whew! Believe it or not, that's all the math. It may seem that there is a lot for your child to remember. There is. But practice using the activities suggested in this chapter (and any others you can think of), and she will be up to speed in no time.

Chapter Four   I GOT A WHAT?!

How to Interpret Your Child's Test Scores

Unfortunately, at the time this book was going to press there was still no official word on how the Grade 4 Mathematics test was going to be scored. The Mathematics test was administered for the first time in June 1999, and if the English Language Arts test of 1999 is any indication, official results for the Math test will not be available until fall 1999.

Internet Information

For the most recent information about both the Elementary Level Tests, check out New York State Education Department's Web site at www.nysed.gov. In addition to some useful general knowledge about the tests, this site shows the fourth-grade English test results for every school and school district in New York.

As for the English Language Arts exam, the key score will be a number between 1 and 4. This number is supposed to show how well your child is progressing on the standards that will be tested on the Regents Examination that students are required to pass to graduate high school. The NYSED breakdown is as follows:

Level 4: Student exceeds performance standards and should get high marks on Regents Examination.

Level 3: Student meets performance standards and with continued effort should pass the Regents Examination.

Level 2: Student needs extra help in order to pass Regents Examination.

Level 1: Student has serious academic deficiencies.

Note that these levels are discussing how well your child should perform on a test that is nine years in his future. Therefore, while a low score can be a cause for concern, it should not necessarily be considered an indication that your child is lagging far behind in his studies and that his education has so far been worthless. Be sure to discuss his scores with the person who is knowledgeable about your child's ability as a student: his teacher. Your child's teacher will provide a better, more complete overview of your child's academic standing than a single-digit score from one standardized test.

It is important that parents keep these scores in perspective. For instance, some parents might be disappointed if their child scores only a 3 instead of a 4. But in fact, only 5 percent of all New York students earned a 4 on the 1999 exam. Considering that 52 percent of all students scored either a 2 or a 1 (both considered nonpassing grades), any child getting a 3 on the English test fared well.

In addition to the main score of 1–4, there will also be a corresponding scaled score ranging from 455 to 800. These scaled scores are just a more precise breakdown of the level 1–4 scores. In other words, since the minimum scaled score needed to receive a Level 3 score is 645, a child who scores 650 and a child who scores a 655 will both receive a Level 3 rating, but the second child's test score is better than the first child's score. These scaled scores allow for a more precise ranking of schools and school districts, but as far as your child is concerned, he passes with a 3 or a 4, and doesn't with a 1 or a 2—*end of story.*

However, it should be noted that in this case, the phrase "end of story" means only "end of discussion on how your child scored on one standardized test." Your child has about a decade of schooling ahead of her. This test should be seen for what it is: an interesting checkpoint along a long highway. Some students who scored a 1 on this test will go on to graduate from prestigious universities with advanced degrees, while other students who scored a 4 will struggle to finish high school. Your child's scores simply highlight where your child needs improvement. And the best person available to make sure your child receives that improvement is currently reading the last sentence of this book.

Ruler   Counters   Pattern Blocks

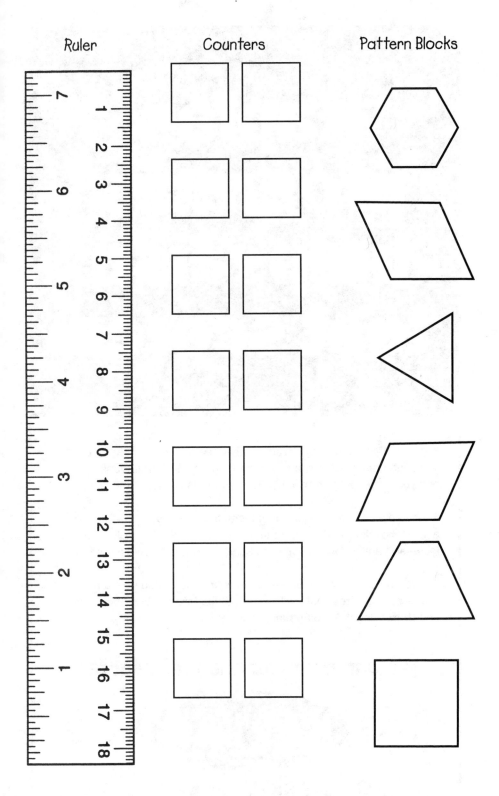

Kaplan programs help raise test scores.

Kaplan's **Basic Skills Intervention Program** offers results: students in our programs achieve an average grade equivalent increase of one year in reading after only 48 hours of instruction.

After Kaplan's **Professional Development Workshops**, teachers gain a greater understanding of testing standards and protocols, plus an increased ability to raise student achievement in the classroom.

Call to find out how Kaplan can help your school prepare for next year's standardized tests with **Basic Skills Intervention Programs** and **Professional Development Workshops**.

We can help you raise test scores.

KAPLAN

1-888-KAPLAN8